This book belongs

_____

The First Woman
MILLIONAIRE
By K.S. Horne

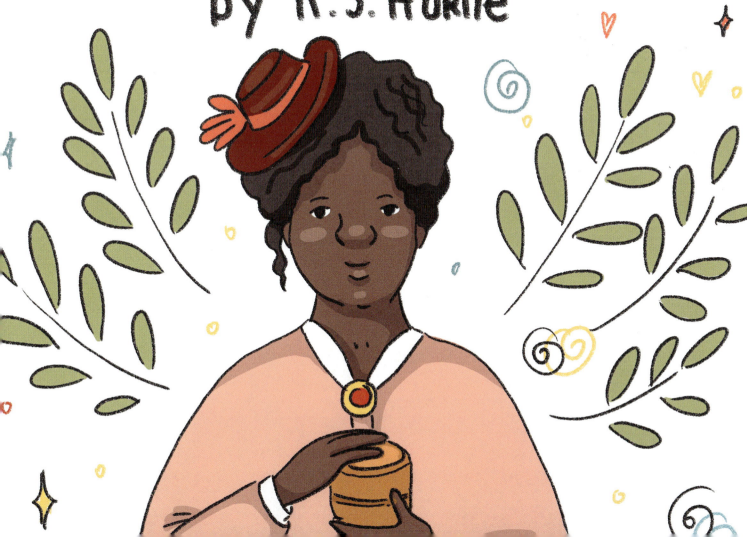

The First Woman Millionaire Was Born in the South

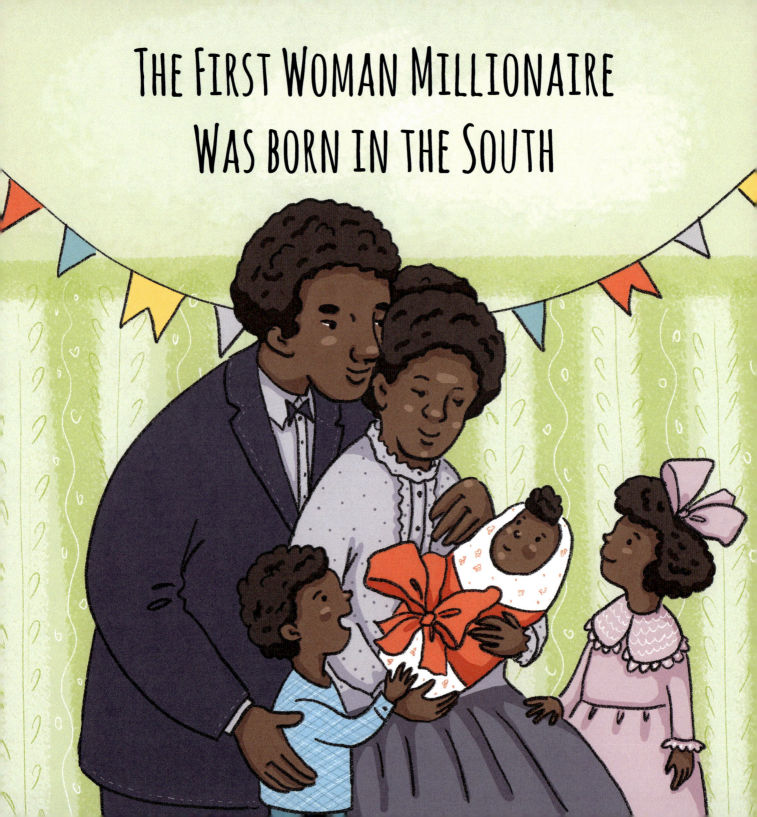

To a family of eight
With no money about

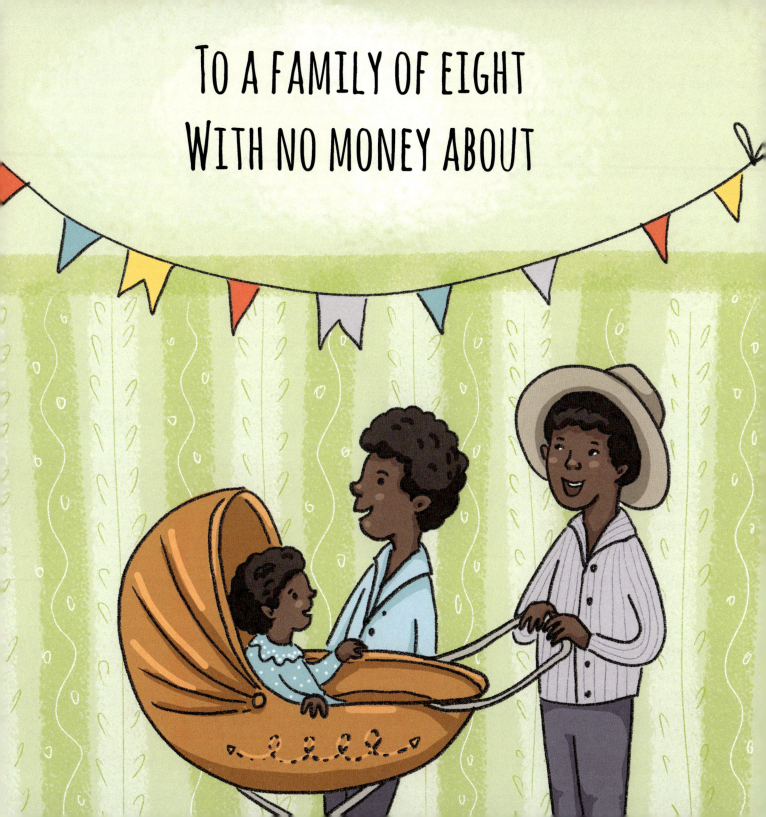

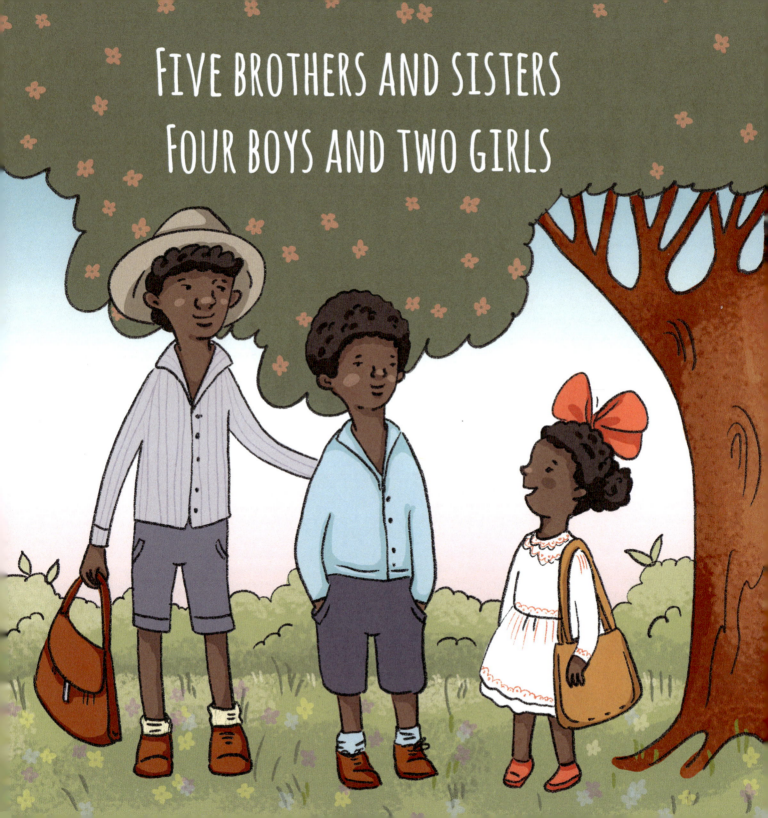

FIVE BROTHERS AND SISTERS
FOUR BOYS AND TWO GIRLS

Young Sarah would one day
Take over the world

WHILE SHE WORKED WASHING CLOTHES
FOR VERY LOW PAY

Sarah heard all the other
Washer women say

Sarah said, "Hey, I know!
I have just what you need."

My natural hair oils
Will make your hair succeed

They used her hair products
And their hair now felt great

She helped millions of women
Feel just like a queen

The first woman millionaire
America had ever seen

So when you think,
"How can I make a million bucks?"
Just help other people
who feel down on their luck

She's Madam CJ Walker
The millionaire queen